Maylyn Murphy's Beginning Easy Singing Lessons

Level 3

Grades 5+

A Complete Voice, Theory, Ear-Training, and Sight-Singing Method for Children

Purvis Atkinson & Maylyn Murphy

ISBN:
ISBN-13:

DEDICATION

To all children who love to sing, especially Samantha.

CONTENTS

INTRODUCTION

Our goal is to teach kids to read and sing music. This is a basic music book for kids grades five and up. It is simple and can be used in the classroom or at home. No difficult terms are used. We have included basics and what is needed to sing the songs in this book. If your child works with a music teacher, he or she will have the best results. But all they need to get started is someone to help them read and, maybe, a small keyboard with a piano key chart.

This book is one of a three book set of beginner song books. Each book starts from scratch, but more information is covered in the higher-level books and in greater detail. This helps students progress according to their age and ability to understand music terms. Level one has music basics for kindergarten through second grade. Level two is a beginning book for grades three through four. It introduces more formal music terms and expanded theory. Level three, for grades five and up, has basics but includes a lot more formal theory. The goal of level three is to provide enough theory so that the student can sing most popular songs.

A great overall book for intermediate young singers is the *Maylyn Murphy Singing and Performance Method.* This book is available from Amazon.com and many other online book stores. We strongly recommend that singers age twelve and under begin with our Beginning Easy Singing Lessons courses.

Note for teachers: We recommend that this book be used in a ten- to twelve- week course.

Enjoy.

LESSON 1

WHAT IS MUSIC

Music

Music has been called "organized sound." The word music comes to us from the Greeks. It refers to Greek Goddesses, who were called *muses*, and who inspired the arts and sciences.

Groups and Patterns

Most music is made up of different sounds which are formed into groups and patterns. These groups and patterns may repeat over and over in a piece of music. This is what catches our attention, unlike noise or people talking, which can be random sound. Music is a little like poetry in the timing of its patterns. It is different in that it is made by people singing or playing instruments like drums, violins, trumpet, guitars and so on.

Sound Groups

Basic music is in patterns of four sounds for each group.

Sound Groups 1.0: count only

Let's count a pattern that has four groups of four sounds or *beats.*

1-2-3-4, 1-2-3-4, 1-2-3-4, 1-2-3-4

Timing Practice 1.2: count and clap

Music is more fun when some of the sounds are different, like the sound of a voice, a drum or a trumptet all in the same song. The timing of all these instruments may seem different. But again all of the sounds will form an overall pattern that fits the song. Let's put beats and claps together. One clap is two beats.

(Hint clap on beats 1 and 3)

Beat 1 – 2 clap, Beat 3 – 4 clap

Beat 1 – 2 clap, Beat 3 – 4 clap

Beat 1 – 2 clap, Beat 3 – 4 clap

Beat 1 – 2 clap, Beat 3 – 4 clap

Sound Group and Timing Practice 1.2: Count, clap, and tap your foot

Here's another change. If this is too easy try alternating when you tap your feet.

Beat 1-2-3-4 clap/tap, clap/tap, clap/tap, clap/tap

Beat 1-2-3-4 clap/tap, clap/tap, clap/tap, clap/tap

Beat 1-2-3-4 clap/tap, clap/tap, clap/tap, clap/tap

Beat 1-2-3-4 clap/tap, clap/tap, clap/tap, clap/tap

Practice Song 1.3

Teacher only: sing and clap using four beats.

A maz ing grace
1-2 3-4 1-2 3-4
How sweet the sound
1-2 3-4 1-2 3-4
That saved a wretch like me
1-2 3-4 1-2 3-4 1 2-3-4
I once was lost
1-2 3-4 1-2 3-4
But now I'm found
1-2 3-4 1-2 3-4
Was blind but now I see
1-2 3-4 1-2 3-4 1 2-3-4

Practice Song 1.4

Teacher and students sing and clap.

A maz ing grace
1-2 3-4 1-2 3-4
How sweet the sound
1-2 3-4 1-2 3-4
That saved a wretch like me
1-2 3-4 1-2 3-4 1 2-3-4
I once was lost
1-2 3-4 1-2 3-4
But now I'm found
1-2 3-4 1-2 3-4
Was blind but now I see
1-2 3-4 1-2 3-4 1 2-3-4

Timing: Fast and Slow

Every song has it's own speed. The timing of exactly how fast or slow a song is can be determined to the second. *Tempo* represents the speed of the song. It tells you how many beats per minute you will use to sing or play your song. Look for the tempo at the start of each song. Here are several of the different speeds:

Speed	Music Term
Very slow	**Largo**
Slow	**Andante**
Medium fast	**Moderato**
Fast	**Allegro**
Very fast	**Presto**

Sounds: Loud and Soft

Songs can be soft like a lullaby or loud like rock music. How loud or soft a song is sung is called *dynamics*. Here are several of the dynamic levels:

Loudness	Music Term
Soft	**Piano**
Medium loud	**Mezzo forte**
Loud	**Forte**
Soft to loud	**Crescendo**
Loud to soft	**Diminuendo**

LESSON 2

MUSIC PARTS

Music Alphabet

There are only seven letters in the music alphabet:

A B C D E F G

Each letter is a certain sound, (tone).

Staff

Music is written on a staff.
A staff has five lines and four spaces. Music notes are written on the lines and spaces.

Each letter has a certain position on a staff.

Treble Clef

A treble clef is placed at the start of a song to tell you the notes that follow will be high notes.

Bass Clef

A bass clef is placed at the start of a song to tell you the notes that follow will be low notes.

Staff Lines for Treble Clef

The staff lines equal certain notes. From bottom to top, they are E, G, B, D, and F. To remember, memorize, Every Good Boy Does Fine

Staff Spaces for Treble Clef

The staff spaces equal certain notes. From bottom to top, they are F, A, C, E. To remember, memorize the word, *FACE*.

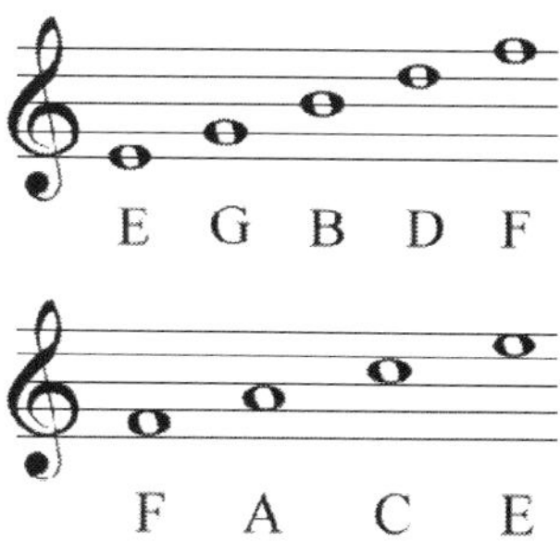

Staff Lines for Bass Clef

From bottom to top, they are G, B, D, F, and A. To remember, memorize, Great Big Dogs Find Apples.

Staff Spaces for Bass Clef

From bottom to top, they are A, C, E, and G. To remember, memorize, All Cows Eat Grass.

Grand Staff

The grand staff shows both treble and bass clef regular notes.

There are notes between regular notes. They are called *sharps* or *flats* and are the black piano keys. Notes that are the same but have different names are also called *Enharmonic* notes. See the black keys below with two different names.

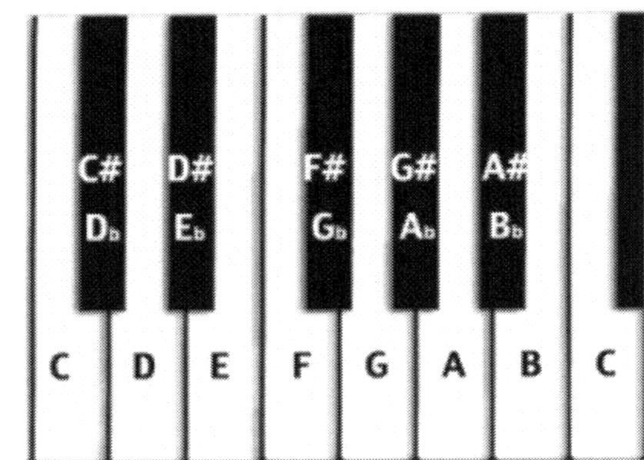

Measure

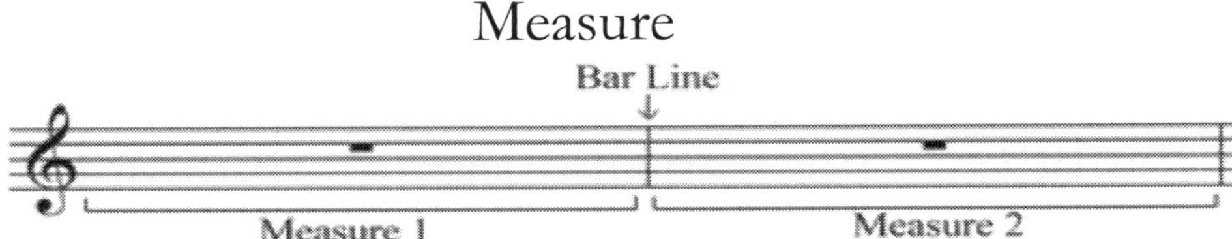

A measure is a section on a staff that is separated by a bar line. Most of the time the number of beats per measure is four. Several measures together make a song.

Time Signatures

The top number tells you how many beats per measure. In this case, there are four. The bottom number tells you which note gets one beat. In this case, it's the quarter note (four= quarter).

Another name for four/four time is common time. The letter C means that a song is using common time.

Three/four time means you have three beats per measure.

Two/four time means you have two beats per measure.

Notes and beats

Each note tells you how many beats it gets.

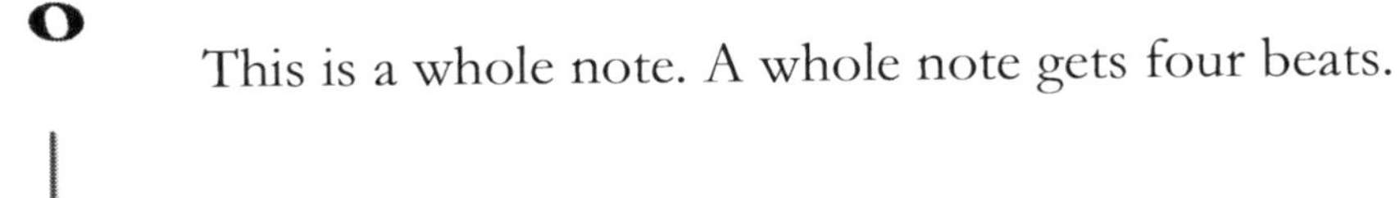

This is a whole note. A whole note gets four beats.

This is a half note. A half note gets two beats.

This is a quarter note. A quarter note gets one beat.

This an eighth note. An eighth note is half of a quarter note. On the right are two eighth notes. Two eighth notes equal one quarter note.

This is a sixteenth note. It takes four sixteenth notes to equal one quarter note.

Dotted Notes and beats

A dotted note gets its normal number of beats plus half that number.

A dotted half note gets three beats.

A dotted quarter note gets one and a half beats.

Other Music Symbols

A *tie* adds two of the same notes together to make one long note. In the example above the note is held for three beats.

A *slur* is when there is a curved line under or over different notes, going from low to high or high to low. This doesn't add extra beats. This tells you to play smooth like a flowing river or another term *legato.*

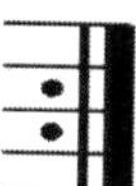

A *repeat* at the end of a song means you sing the whole song twice.

A *whole rest:* stop singing for four beats.

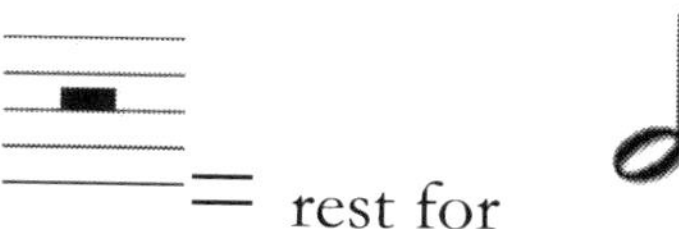

A *half rest:* stop singing for two beats.

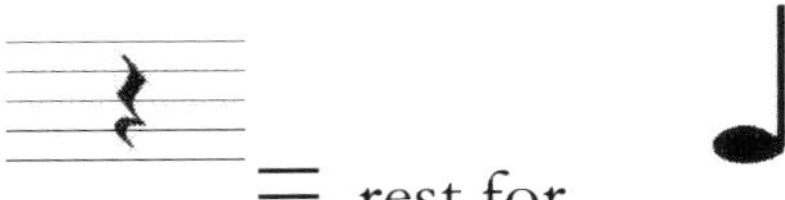

A *quarter rest:* stop singing for one beat.

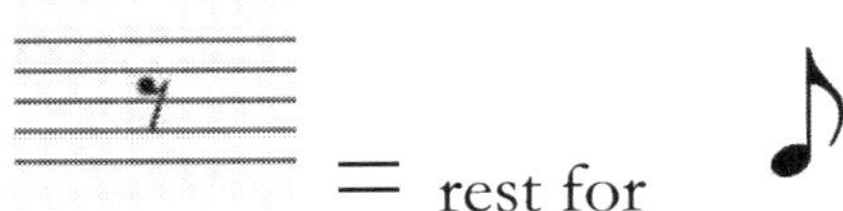

An eighth rest: stop singing for half a beat.

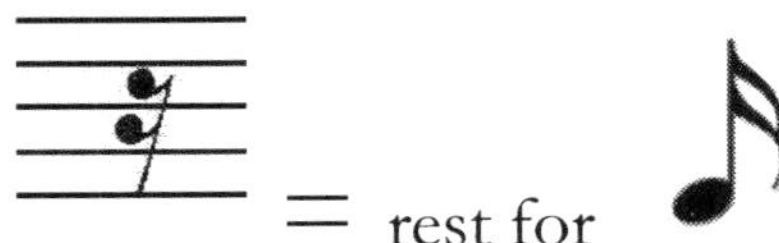

A sixteenth rest: stop singing for one fourth of a beat.

LESSON 3

HOW TO SING

Breathing

Learning to sing is about learning how to breathe properly. You will be able to control your voice and it will sound best when your breathing is correct. Here are some exercises to improve your voice and breathing.

Breathing Practice 3.0

1. Stand up straight. (straight but relaxed, not stiff)

2. Hold your head up. (not too high, you should be looking straight ahead)

3. Place your right hand over the center of your chest at the bottom bone.
   Here you will notice that your stomach will expand slightly as you breathe in and it will relax as you breathe out.

4. Take a deep breath for four counts and fill your lungs.
   Imagine you can see the air going into your nose, down your throat, in to the top of your lungs, and going all the way down to the bottom of your lungs.

5. Breathe out for four beats while making the sound *aaaaah.*
   Now imagine the air leaving your lungs starting from the very bottom, then up to the top of your lungs, through your throat, and finally out your mouth.

If you are doing this right you should feel the sound starting in your chest and passing through your throat and out your mouth as your lungs empty. To make it simple your chest should vibrate!

Repeat this practice several times. It is also a good daily exercise for future singing stars.

Singing Basics

Breathe

Breathing correctly will help you become a better singer. It will help you hold notes longer and sing louder. Practice your breathing exercises every time you sing.

Posture

In order to get the best and strongest tone from your voice you must have your body in a strong position. To do this, sit up or stand up with your back straight, shoulders back, rest your weight evenly on both hips or both feet. Make sure you are singing from a position of power. You will sing better this way.

Control

Control is what you learn from practicing your breathing exercises. It helps your vocal *dynamics*. It also allows you to learn to hold a note without running out of air.

Don't strain

It should not hurt when you sing. If you feel yourself straining you should stop and rest. Straining means you are trying to sing too high or pushing too hard. It also can mean that you are not breathing correctly. Either way the results are the same. You need to take it easy.

Head voice

Your "head voice" is a sound you make when you are not fully using your lungs to breath and sing. As you sing you will feel this more in your head than chest. This is natural and necessary for reaching those really high notes. To use your head voice correctly you must breathe properly, as I have mentioned before.

Chest voice

Your "chest voice" is your lower vocal range. When you reach for those low notes you will notice more vibration in your chest. You must also breathe correctly to get the best sound from your chest voice.

Pitch

There are eighty-eight keys (notes) on a piano. As you move from left to right the sound of the keys become higher and higher. So the lowest note is the one farthest to the left and the highgest note on the piano is the one farthest to the right. Each note has it's own sound and this is called *pitch.* When someone says you are on or off key they mean that you are not singing the correct note. They are talking about your pitch. This next exercise will help you with your pitch.

Pitch Practice 3.1

(Teacher: perform this practice starting at middle C. Repeat for students as needed.)

Teacher only:

Play a C and sing *do* for four beats
Play a D and sing *re* for four beats
Play an E and sing *mi* for four beats
Play a F and sing *fa* for four beats

o =*do*

o =*re*

o =*mi*

o =*fa*

Pitch Practice 3.2

Teacher, play and sing the above exercise with your students. Repeat as needed.

O =*do*

O =*re*

O =*mi*

O =*fa*

Pitch Practice 3.3

Teacher only:

Play a G and sing *sol* for four beats
Play an A and sing *la* for four beats
Play a B and sing *ti* for four beats
Play a C and sing *do* for four beats

O =*sol*

O =*la*

O =*ti*

O =*do*

Pitch Practice 3.4

Teacher, play and sing the above exercise with your students. Repeat as needed.

o =*sol*

o =*la*

o =*ti*

o =*do*

Pitch Practice 3.5

Teacher only:

Play a C and sing *do* for four beats
Play a D and sing *re* for four beats
Play an E and sing *mi* for four beats
Play a F and sing *fa* for four beats
Play a G and sing *sol* for four beats
Play an A and sing *la* for four beats
Play a B and sing *ti* for four beats
Play a C and sing *do* for four beats

Pitch Practice 3.6

Teacher, play and sing the above exercise with your students. Repeat as needed.

O =*do*

O =*re*

O =*mi*

O =*fa*

O =*sol*

O =*la*

O =*ti*

O =*do*

LESSON 4

SCALES AND INTERVALS

Scales

A scale is a group of musical notes in order by pitch.

A group of eight notes in order is called an *octave.* The word octave means eight. If, for example, the first note is C, then the last note is also C but seven notes higher. On a piano you can play many octaves from low to high. It is also easy to see octave patterns on a piano keyboard.

If you study scales, you will learn the proper order of notes. There are many scales. We will cover the most common.

The easiest and most well known scale is C major. The other common scales we will cover are F, G, D, and A major. There are many other scales which we will cover in other books, but let's start at the beginning with C,F, G, D, and A major.

Octave

Intervals

In order to understand how a scale is made you must first learn about the spacing between notes or interval. An *interval* is the distance between two notes. The interval between most notes is called a *whole step*. For the spacing between E to F and B to C, the interval is only a *half step*. This is very important, and you will see why on the next page. For now, remember the interval distance for the notes in the scale below.

Overview of Whole Step and Half Step Concept

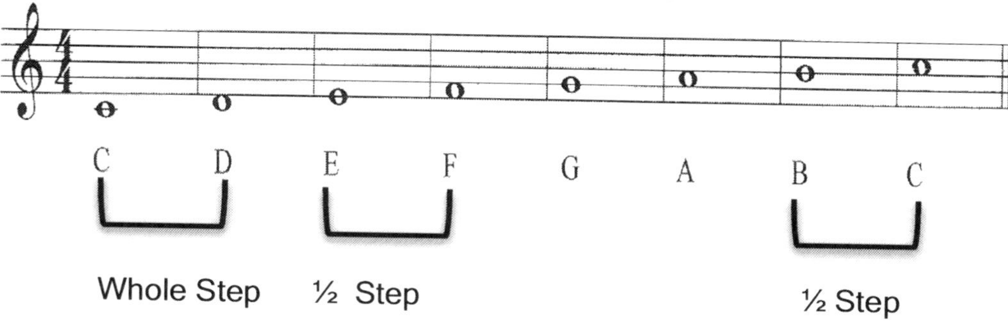

Each note in an octave can be identified by a number or reference term. The *root or unison* is the first note. The notes that follow are numbered *second*, *third*, *fourth* and so on. The final note in the scale is called the *octave*. This is important to learn now and is necessary if you go on to study music in intermediate and advanced courses.

C Scale Interval Relationships to Root/Unison

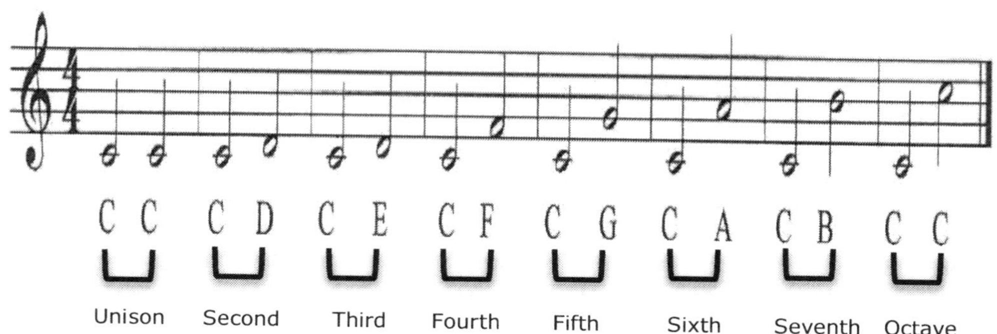

Sharps and Flats

When the interval between notes is a whole step, you have room for another note. If you are going from a lower to a higher note, the note in-between is called a *sharp*. If you are going from a lower higher note to a lower note, the note in-between is called a *flat*. As you can see in the examples below, the same note can be called a sharp or a flat. This makes music fun. It is also easy to understand as you practice reading music and see how these notes appear in songs.

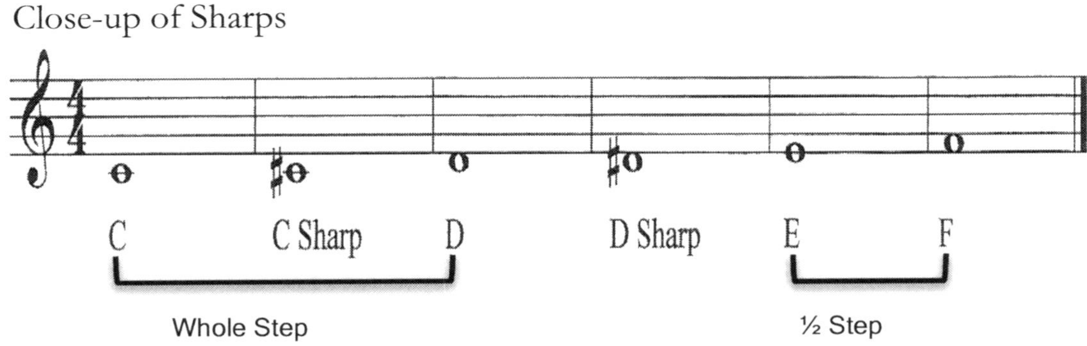

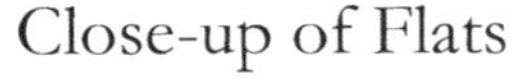

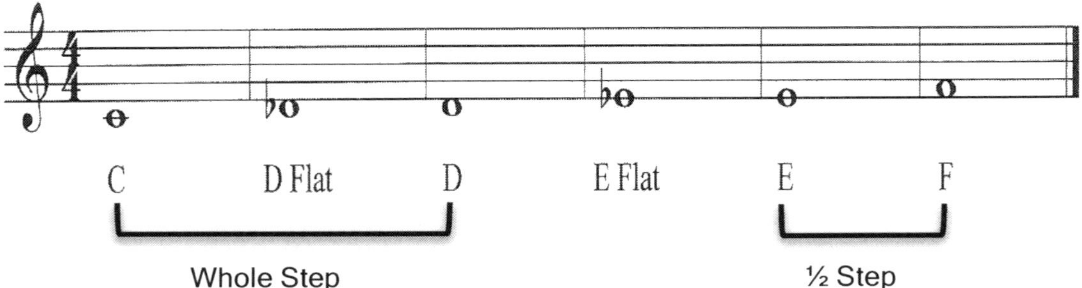

These are all of the notes that can appear as sharps. Note B and E sharp are really C and F in disguise. In our earlier discussion on intervals, we noted that there is only a half step between B to C and E to F. B and E sharp are the exceptions.

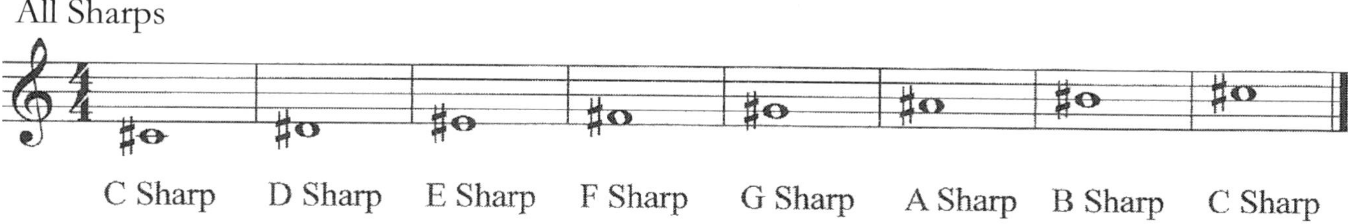

These are all of the notes that can appear as flats. The same exception for B and E also applies to flat notes. In this case, C and F flat are really B and E in disguise. If all of this is getting confusing, study the keyboard diagram below.

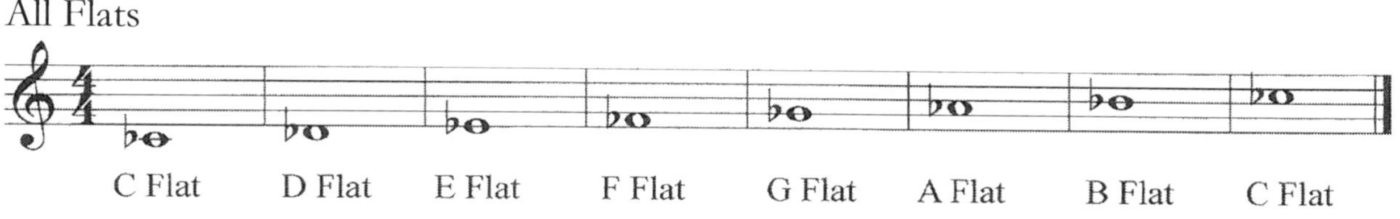

Okay, here's a piano diagram which shows the notes in the C scale. Notice how the sharps and flats are labeled. Hopefully this clears up any confusion with the exceptions for sharps and flats. Remember, notes that are the same but have different names are also called *enharmonic* notes. See the black keys below with two different names.

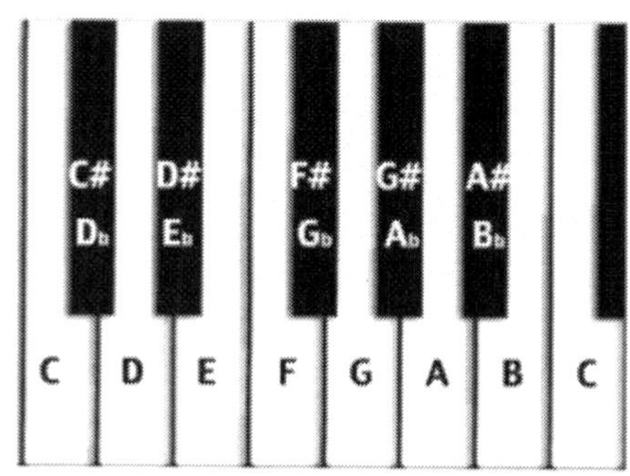

C Major Scale

Teacher, sing and play the C Scale:

Now, the teacher plays and students sing the C Scale in half notes.

Teacher plays and students sing *do re mi*:

Teacher, sing and play the C scale in quarter notes:

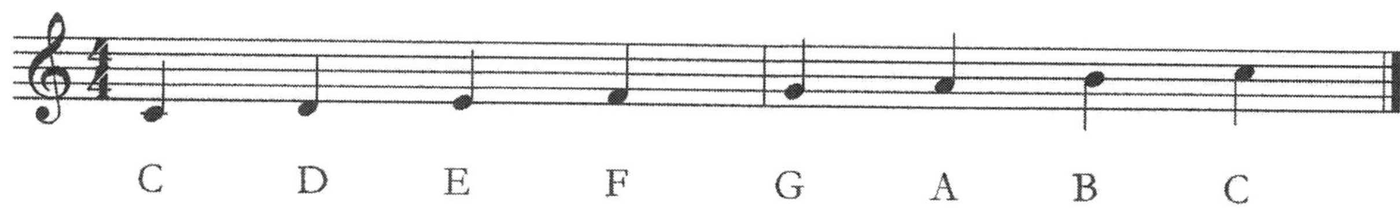

Teacher plays and students sing *do re mi*:

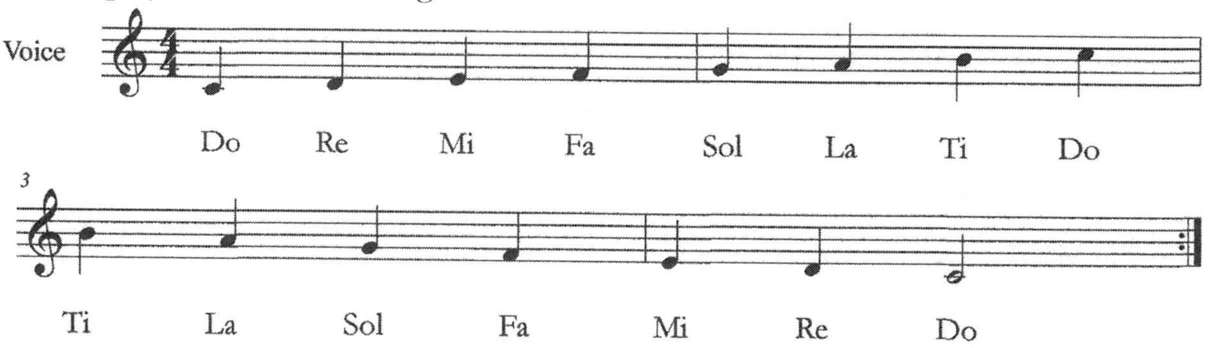

F Major

Note F major has one flat note. The symbol after the treble clef shows which note is flat.

Teacher, sing and play the F Scale:

Now, the teacher plays and students sing the F Scale in half notes.

Teacher plays and students sing *do re mi*:

Teacher, sing and play F major scale in quarter notes:

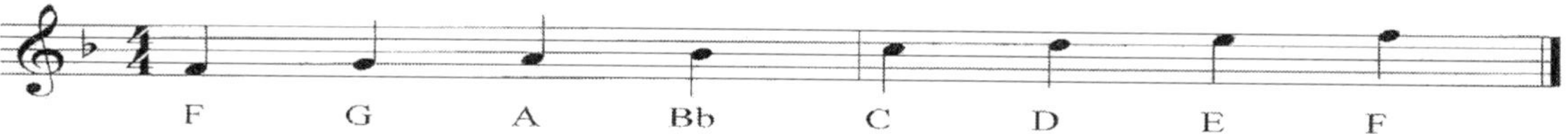

Teacher plays and students sing *do re mi*:

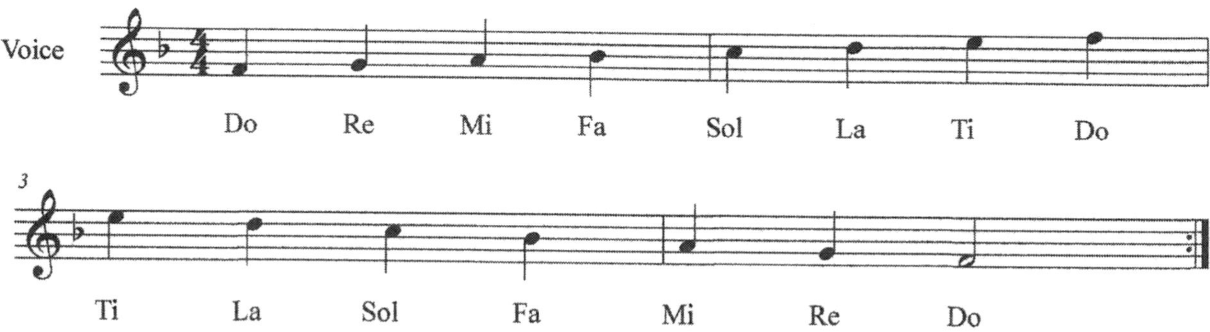

G Major

Note G major has one sharp note. The symbol after the treble clef shows which note is sharp.

Teacher, sing and play the G Scale:

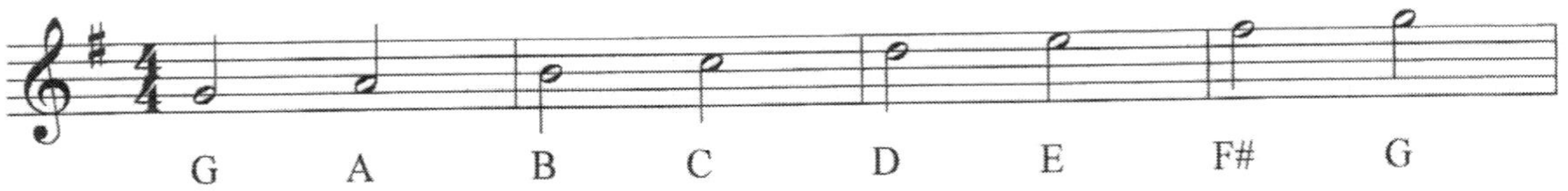

Now, the teacher plays and students sing the G Scale in half notes.

Teacher plays and students sing *do re mi*:

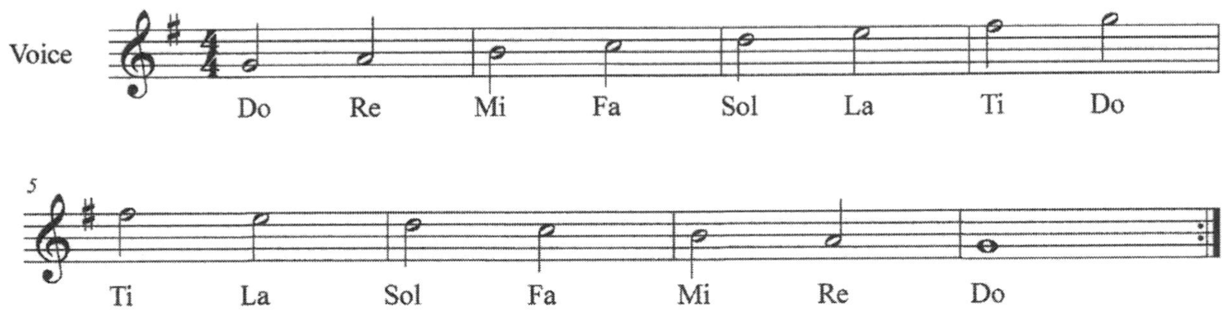

Teacher, sing and play G major scale in quarter notes:

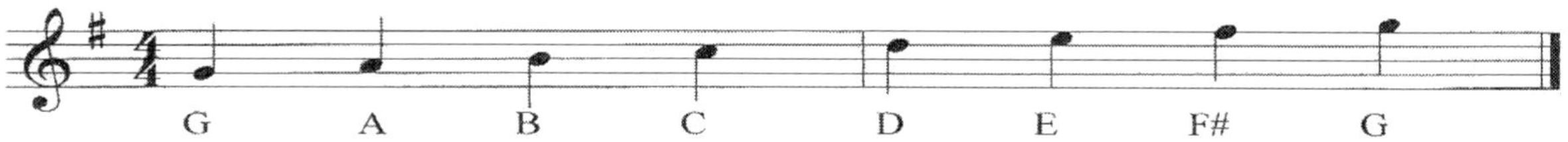

Teacher plays and students sing *do re mi*:

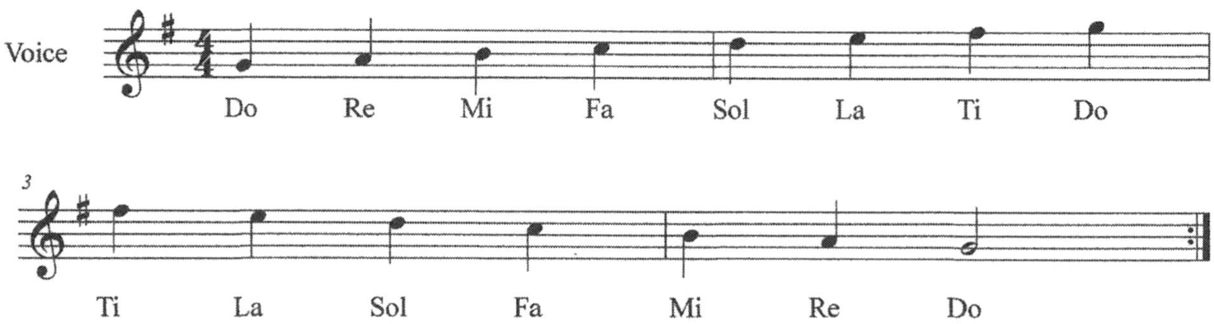

D Major

Note D major has two sharp notes. The symbol after the treble clef shows which notes are sharp.

Teacher, sing and play the D Scale:

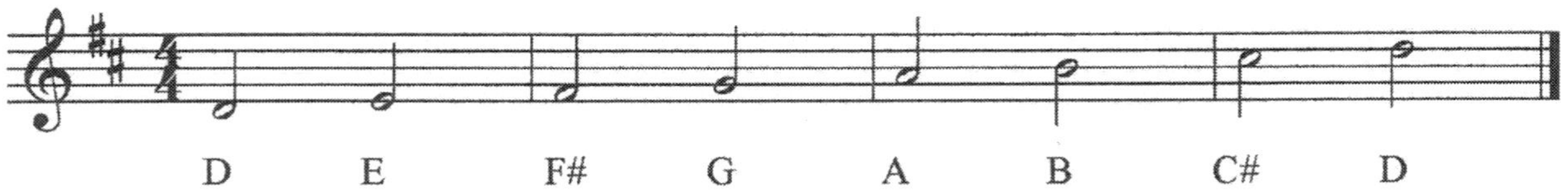

Now, the teacher plays and students sing the D Scale in half notes.

Teacher plays and students sing *do re mi*:

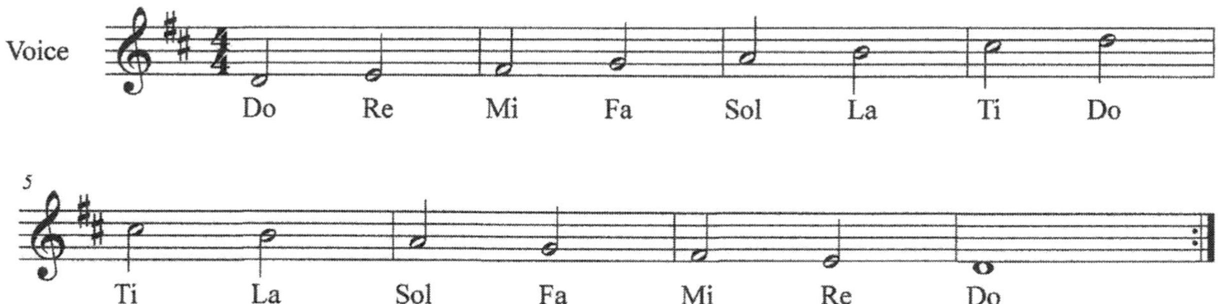

Teacher, sing and play D major scale in quarter notes:

Teacher plays and students sing *do re mi*:

A Major

Note A major has three sharp notes. The symbol after the treble clef shows which notes are sharp.

Teacher, sing and play the A scale:

Now, the teacher plays and students sing the A scale in half notes.

Teacher plays and students sing *do re mi:*

Teacher, sing and play A major scale in quarter notes:

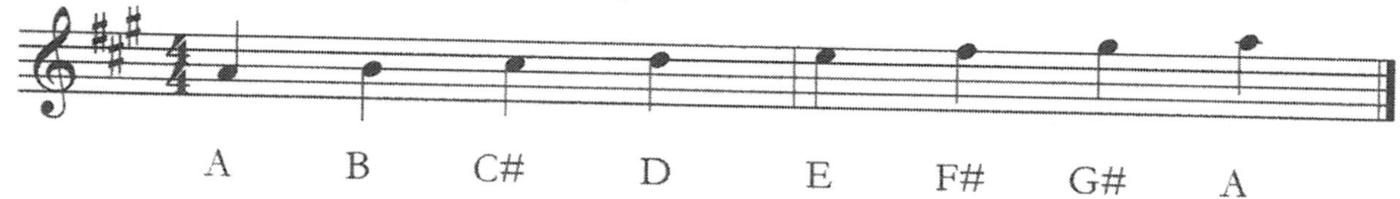

Teacher plays and students sing *do re mi:*

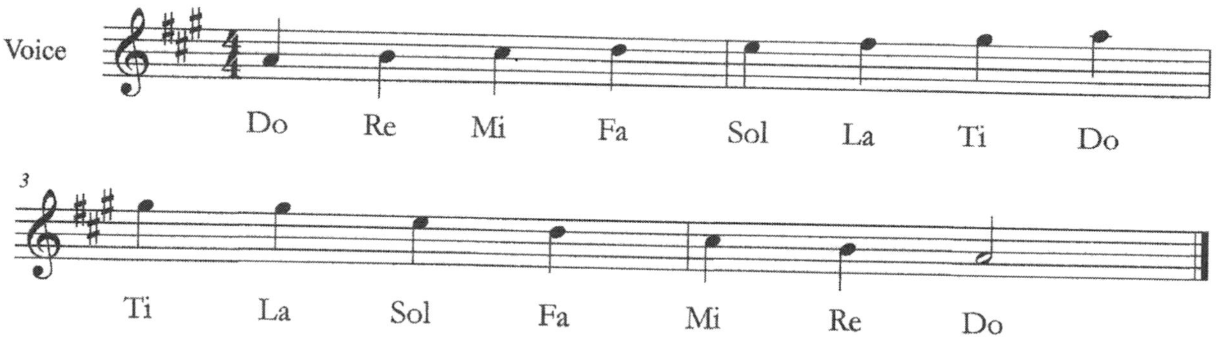

LESSON 5

WHAT MAKES A SONG

Recipe for a song

What is it about your favorite song that makes you sing or dance? I bet it's a bunch of things. We will discuss many of these in this chapter.

Lyrics

The words in a song are called lyrics. Like a poem, lyrics mostly rhyme. Different from a poem certain sections of a lyrics are repeated over and over. That's the part of the lyrics we get hooked on.

Melody

When you sing lyrics most of the time you are singing notes that make up the melody. A melody is a series of tones that form a unit with a beginning, middle, and end. Melody goes high and low, it takes a repeating shape-pattern and it moves from one point to the another.

Dynamics

The loudness or softness of a song is called dynamics. You can have a range of loud and soft notes all in the same song. Dynamics add expression and emotion to a song.

Rhythm

Rhythm deals with musical time and has several parts. The first is the accenting of beats. As you listen to a song you may notice the drummer or bassist playing some beats harder or louder than others. The second facet of rhythm is meter. This basically refers to the number of beats in a measure. The last part of rhythm is tempo, that is, how slowly or quickly a song is played. Tempo is measured in beats per minute (bpm). The fastest tempo is prestissimo, which is about two hundred bpm, the slowest is largo, which is forty to sixty bpm. The five most popular tempos were covered in chapter one.

Harmony

Harmony adds depth and color to melody. To achieve harmony, two or more notes must be sung or played together. Harmony can be an agreeable sound-consonance or a harsh sound-dissonance.

Song sections

The primary sections of a song are the verse (A), chorus (B), and bridge (C). Let's discuss the ABCs of form because they are commonly used to describe popular song structure.

Verse

The verse is considered the A section. The verse of a song has been compared to a stanza or section of a poem. Each time the verse comes up it may be slightly different. The words of the verse move the song along.

Chorus

The chorus is the B section. The chorus or hook is the part of the song we tend to remember best, mostly because the chorus is the part of the song most often repeated.

Bridge

The bridge is the C section. It allows the song to change, normally from middle to end. Like a bridge over water, it allows us to move from one place to the next.

LESSON 6

SOLFEGE

Solfege

Why Solfege

Solfeggio is the best and oldest method that singers use to improve their voices. You have already used it in this book, and maybe even before, without knowing it. Every time you sing "Do Re Mi" you are doing solfege. It seems so simple, and yet it's such a powerful tool. The practice of solfege goes back several hundred years. It was designed to provide a method to help choirs sing in tune. Today you can use it to help you learn to stay in tune and also to recognize different notes. When you practice solfege there are two parts: singing and listening to how you sound. This is called *ear training* and you cannot be a good or great singer without it.

The exercises in this chapter should be practiced daily. They should also be apart of your warm-up routine before you sing a song. We have included solfege exercises for the five scales you have learned. There are three slightly different versions to keep your attention.

C Major
Version 1

F Major
Version 2

G Major
Version 3

D Major
Version 1

A Major
Version 2

LESSON 7

AMERICA THE BEAUTIFUL

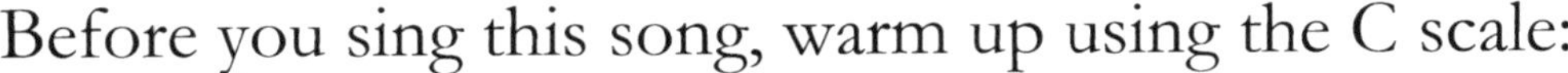

Before you sing this song, warm up using the C scale:

Important Items:

Eighth Notes

This an eighth note. An eighth note is half of a quarter note.
On the right are two eighth notes. Two eighth notes equal one quarter note.

Dotted quarter note

A dotted quarter note gets one and a half beats.

Quarter note rest

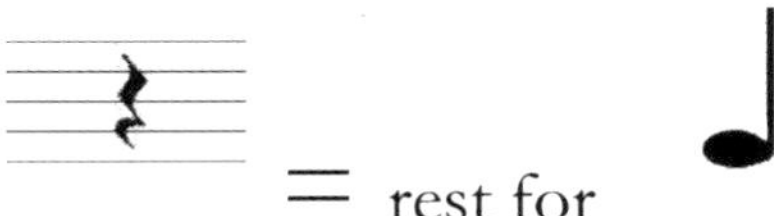

A quarter note rest. Stop singing for one beat.

Second and Third Verses

Almost every song has more than one verse. In "America the Beautiful" the first verse is written directly underneath the notes. The second and third verses are written separately at the bottom of the song. To complete the song, you must sing all three verses.

America the Beautiful

2. O beautiful for pilgrim feet
Whose stern impassioned stress
A thoroughfare of freedom beat
Across the wilderness!
America! America!
God mend thine every flaw,
Confirm thy soul in self-control,
Thy liberty in law!

3. O beautiful for heroes proved
In liberating strife.
Who more than self their country loved
And mercy more than life!
America! America!
May God thy gold refine
Till all success be nobleness
And every gain divine!

LESSON 8

THIS LITTLE LIGHT OF MINE

Before you sing this song, warm up using the G scale:

This Little Light of Mine

2. Always in my heart,
I'm gonna let it shine.
Always in my heart,
I'm gonna let it shine.
Always in my heart,
I'm gonna let it shine.
Let it shine, let it shine, let it shine.

3.Everywhere I go,
I'm gonna let it shine.
Everywhere I go,
I'm gonna let it shine.
Everywhere I go,
I'm gonna let it shine.
Let it shine, let it shine, let it shine.

LESSON 9

SHENANDOAH

Before you sing this song, warm up using the F scale

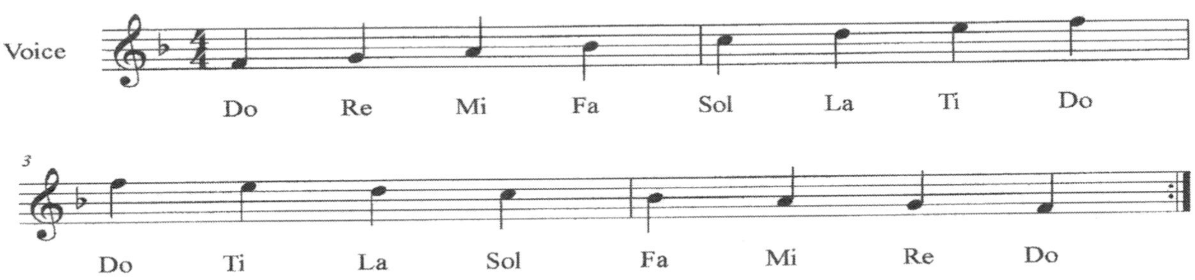

Important Items:

Tie

A *tie* adds two of the same notes together to make one long note. In the example above the note is held for three beats.

Slur

A *slur* is when there is a curved line under or over different notes, going from low to high or high to low. This doesn't add extra beats. This tells you to play smooth like a flowing river or another term *legato*.

Shenandoah

American Folksong

Andante and mezzo forte **Arranged by: Maylyn Murphy**

2. Shenadoah, I love you truly,
Away, you rollin' river.
O Shenadoah, I'm bound to leave you.
Away, I'm bound away, 'cross the wide Missouri.

LESSON 10

C.C. RIDER

Before you sing this song, warm up using the D scale:

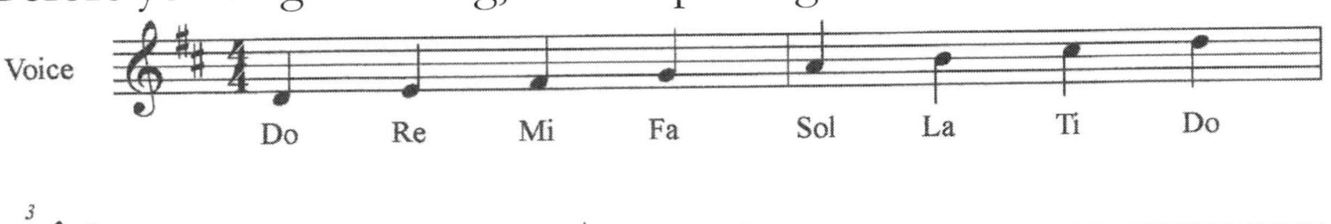

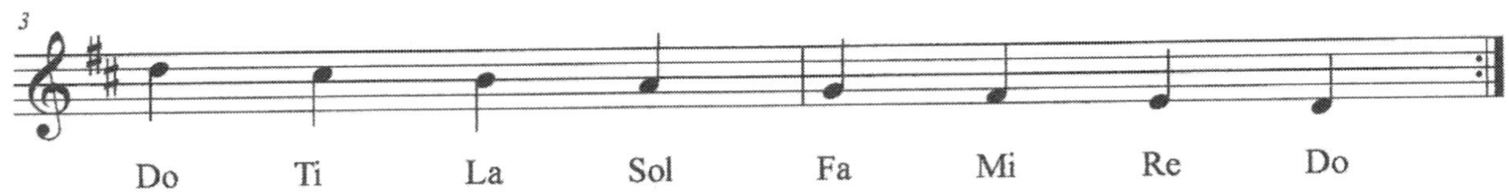

Important Items:

Cut Time

Cut time is four/four time cut in half. It is also called two/two time. It means that there are two half notes per measure, and each half note gets one beat.

Half rest

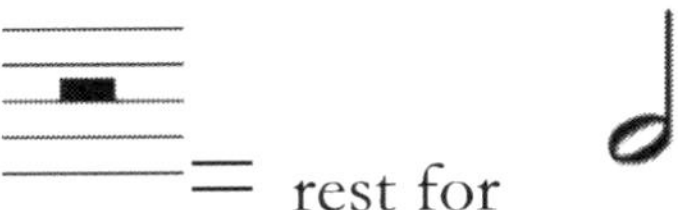

A half rest. Stop singing for two beats.

Natural Note

A natural note is not sharp or flat. The symbol is used when a composer wants to play a regular note that is different from the main key of a song.

C C Rider

Traditional

Allegro and forte

Arranged by: Maylyn Murphy

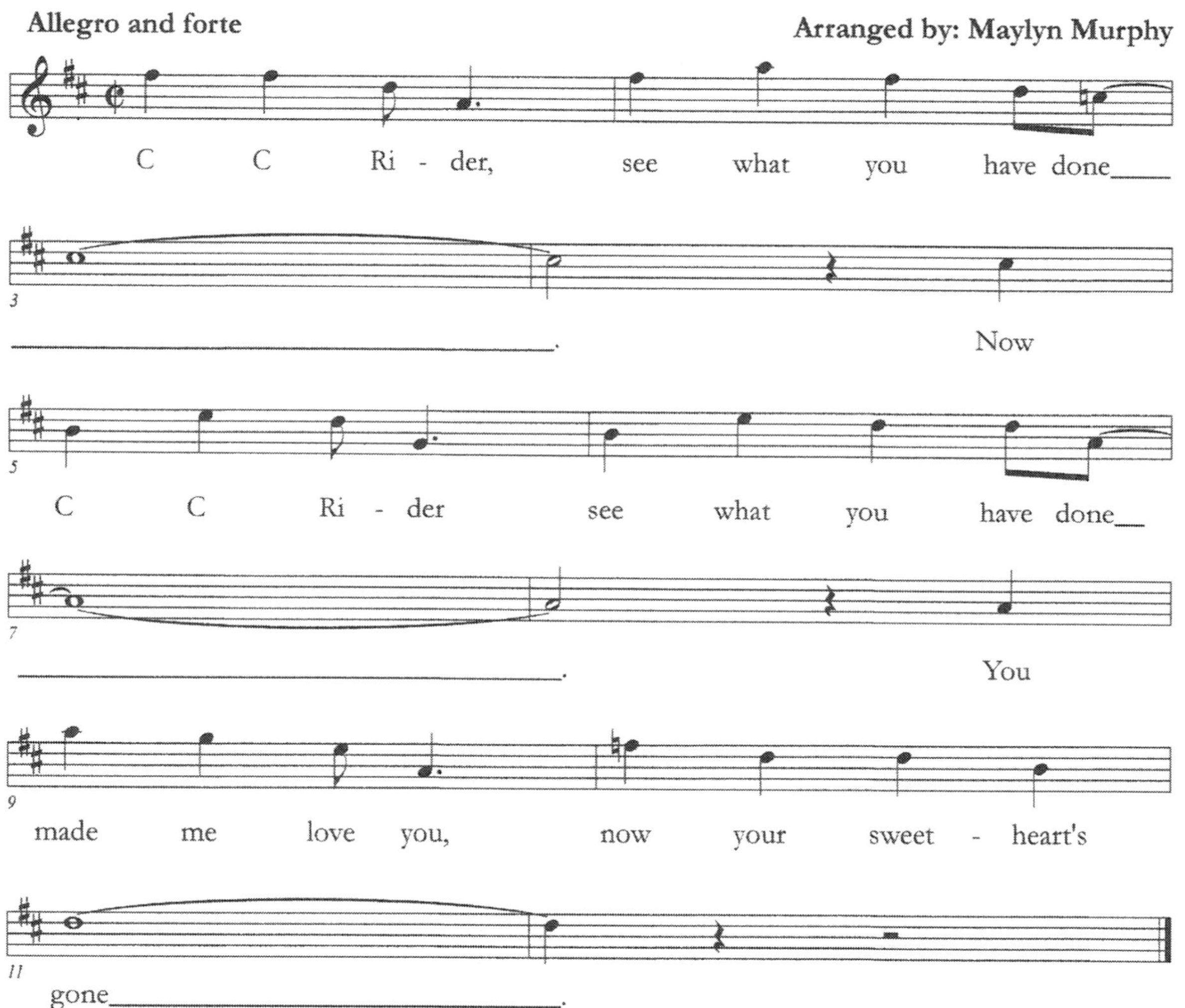

2. My home's on the water, I don't like no land at all.
My home's on the water, I don't like no land at all.
I'd rather be gone than stay and be your dog.

3. I'm going away babe, sure you don't want to go.
I'm going away babe, sure you don't want to go.
Well I'm leaving this town, not coming back no more.

LESSON 11

WADE IN THE WATER

Before you sing this song, warm up using the A scale:

Wade In The Water

Spiritual

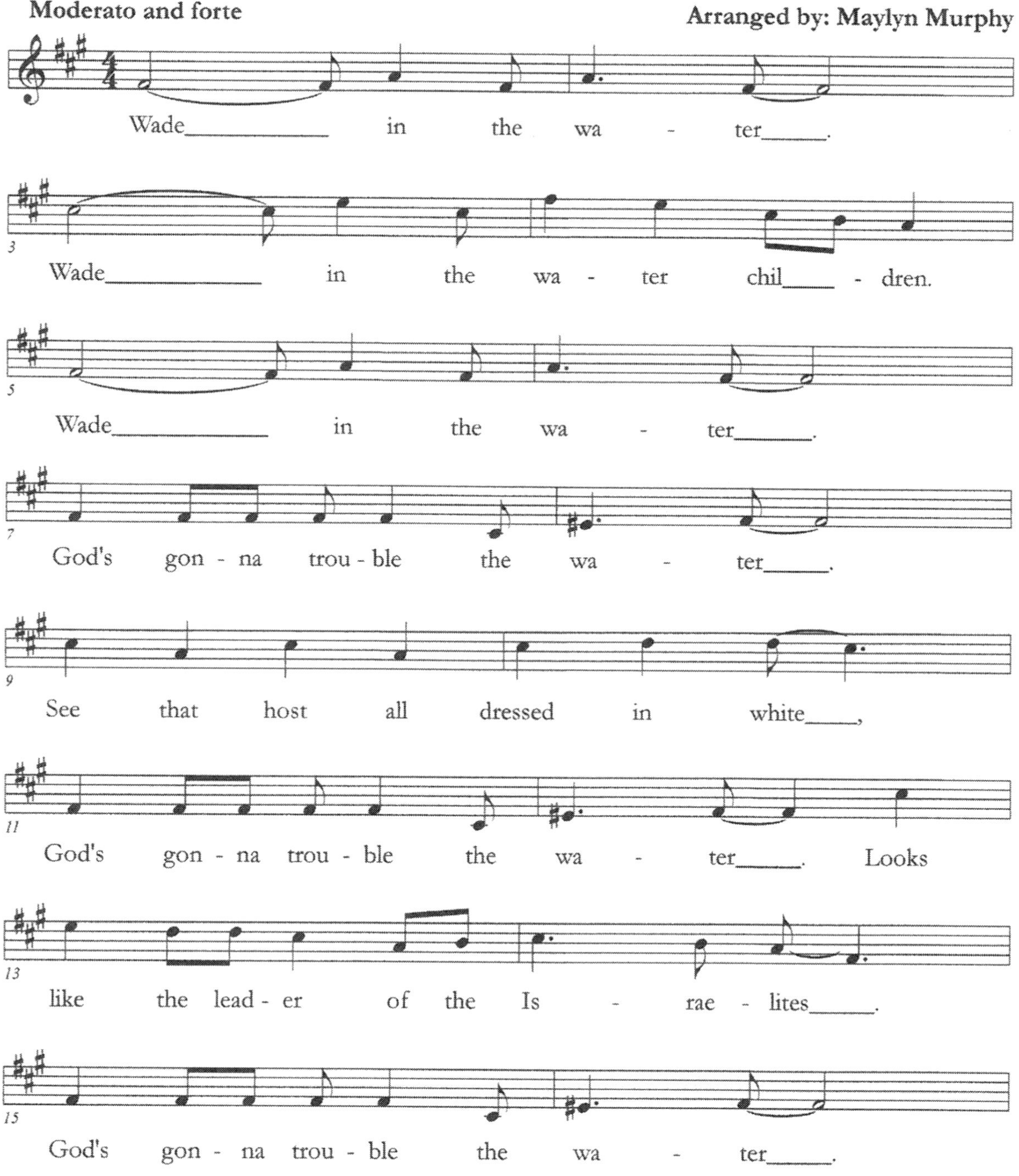

2. Who are those children dressed in red?
God's gonna trouble the water.
Must be the children that Moses led.
God's gonna trouble the water.

3. Jordan's water is chilly and cold.
God's gonna trouble the water.
It chills the body, but not the soul.
God's gonna trouble the water.

4. If you get there before I do.
God's gonna trouble the water.
Tell my all my friends I'm coming too.
God's gonna trouble the water.

ABOUT THE AUTHOR

Maylyn Murphy is an accomplished singer, songwriter, bandleader and teacher. She graduated from Berklee College of Music in Boston. Maylyn has performed with some of the biggest names in music today. Her latest CD *Body and Soul* is available for download from iTunes or CD Baby. Visit her at www.maylynmurphy.com and on her Facebook pages at Maylyn Murphy or Music Nation Academy.

Purvis Atkinson is Maylyn's dad. He is a retired navy veteran and a music lover. Purvis writes music and other inspirational books for young people. Look for his latest books on his Facebook page or Amazon and other online book retailers.